THE SUPER SCIENCE BOOK OF WEATHER

Kay Davies and Wendy Oldfield

Weather Knows What Next

Weather comes and weather goes
With freezing fingers or red hot toes,
You think you know what to expect
But you never know what's coming next.

Illustrations by Frances Lloyd

Wayland

Titles in the Super Science series

Light
Our Bodies
Time
Weather

The Super Science Book of Weather

This book explains how the weather happens. In doing so, it takes a look at all sorts of subjects – the world around us, times gone by, weather lore and myths, how materials behave, life on earth, how things work and the earth in space.

Whether you choose to dip into this book and answer your own questions, or try out some of the simple activities, or sit down and read it from cover to cover, the *Super Science Book of Weather* will show you that science can be fascinating.

First published in 1992 by Wayland (Publishers) Ltd
61 Western Road, Hove, East Sussex, BN3 1JD, England

© Copyright 1992 Wayland (Publishers) Ltd
© Copyright *Weather Knows What Next* 1992 Kay Davies

British Library Cataloguing in Publication Data
Davies, Kay
  Weather.—(Super Science Series)
  I. Title II. Oldfield, Wendy
  III. Gordon, Martin IV. Series
  551.6

ISBN 0 7502 0425 7

Typeset by Dorchester Typesetting Group Ltd
Printed and bound by L.E.G.O. in Italy

Series Editor: Cally Chambers
Designer: Loraine Hayes Design
Consultant: Graham Peacock, Senior Lecturer, Centre for Science Education, Sheffield City Polytechnic

Picture acknowledgements

Illustrations by Frances Lloyd.
Cover illustration by Martin Gordon.

Photographs by permission of: J Allan Cash 5, 11; Cephas 24; Bruce Coleman Ltd. 13 bottom (Taylor), 17 bottom, 21 (Myers), 22 bottom (Lankinen); Ecoscene 23, 26; Environmental Picture Library 29 (Holmes); Eye Ubiquitous 8; PHOTRI 22 top, 27 bottom; Science Photo Library 19, 27 top; Tony Stone Worldwide 4, 13 top, 16, 17 top, 18, 25; Werner Forman Archive 28.

CONTENTS

WEATHER

People always want to know what the weather will be like. They may be planning a picnic or barbecue, or deciding how to travel to work or whether to carry an umbrella. They can listen to weather forecasts on the TV and radio. The forecasts are updated all the time, just as weather conditions are always changing and developing.

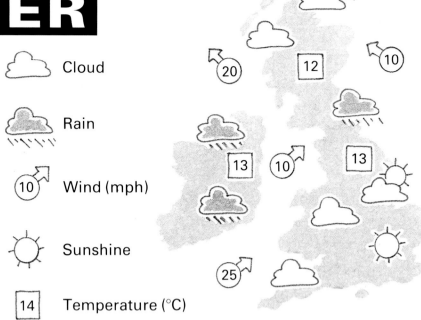

Cloud

Rain

Wind (mph)

Sunshine

14 Temperature (°C)

▲ A weather map in a newspaper can tell people what kind of weather to expect. A few simple symbols make it easy to understand.

Weather is made up of the day-to-day changes in the atmosphere around us. We see and feel the weather in the wind, rain, sunshine, frost or fog.

◄ The weather can change quickly – a bright, sunny day can suddenly be clouded over by a dark thunderstorm. Have you ever started a country walk in sunny weather and seen a heavy rain shower on its way?

ATMOSPHERE

The earth is surrounded by air, which is a mixture of gases that makes up the atmosphere. Nitrogen and oxygen, with a small amount of carbon dioxide as well as other gases and water vapour, are all mixed up together. Small amounts of dust and dirt are found too.

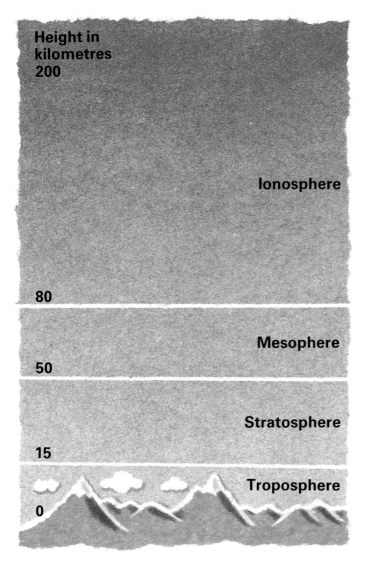

Height in kilometres
200

Ionosphere

80

Mesophere

50

Stratosphere

15

Troposphere

0

Although air is made up of gases, it still has weight. The weight of the atmosphere pushing down on the earth is called air pressure. It pushes in all directions – up, down and sideways – so we never notice it. Air pressure is greater nearer the surface of the earth because there is more air pushing down from above.

▲ The atmosphere is hundreds of kilometres thick and is arranged in layers. The one nearest the earth is about 15 km deep and is called the troposphere. It contains nearly all the air and water vapour in the atmosphere. It is where the weather happens.

▲ Air pressure patterns in the atmosphere are changing all the time. With these changes come variations in the weather. A barometer shows changes in air pressure and what kind of weather to expect.

SUN RAYS

The sun's rays travel through the ▶ atmosphere. They warm the air and the surface of the land and sea. Heat from the land and sea is given out again and helps warm the air around us. Some heat escapes back into space but a lot is trapped in the atmosphere and keeps the earth warm. This is known as the greenhouse effect.

Not all parts of the world receive the same amount of the sun's heat. Because the earth is round, the sun's rays strike the curved surface at different angles. Near the Poles they have further to travel through the same thickness of atmosphere. Lots of heat is absorbed before it can reach the surface and even when the sunlight reaches earth, it is spread thinly over a wide area. Areas near the Equator get the sun's direct rays all year round and so are warmer than regions nearest the Poles. ▼

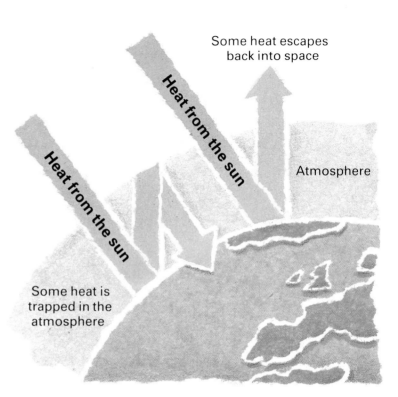

Some heat escapes back into space

Heat from the sun

Heat from the sun

Atmosphere

Some heat is trapped in the atmosphere

Position on the earth's surface is not the only factor that influences the temperature of a place. Winds and ocean currents may cool land down or bring in warm air. The higher the altitude of a place, the cooler it is likely to be. The amount of cloud cover will have an affect too and temperatures will usually be warmer in the day than at night. Weather fronts passing over can bring warm or cold air masses with them.

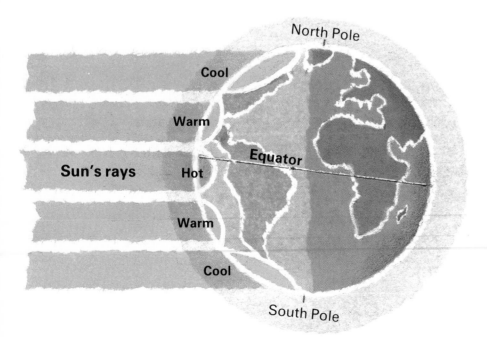

North Pole

Cool

Warm

Sun's rays

Equator

Hot

Warm

Cool

South Pole

CLIMATE

Climate is made up of the regular weather patterns that an area has over a long period of time. The kind of climate a place has will be influenced by winds, ocean currents, height of the land, amount of sunlight reaching the place and many other factors.

Regions of the world are often described according to the kind of climate they have. Usually they are described in terms of their temperature and rainfall patterns. There are many climates, but three main kinds are often picked out. ▼

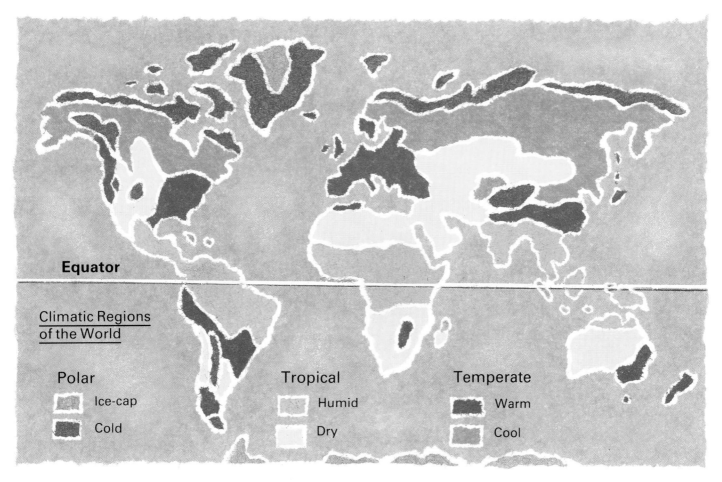

Equator

Climatic Regions
of the World

Polar
Ice-cap
Cold

Tropical
Humid
Dry

Temperate
Warm
Cool

Lands around the Equator are usually hot all year round and have high rainfall. They are said to have a tropical climate.

The Polar climate of the Arctic and Antarctic is much colder and often has snow all year round, even during the summer.

Between the Equator and the Poles there are many different types of climate. Many of them have winter and summer seasons and the regions are said to have a temperate climate. The summers are generally warm and dry, and the winters are cold and wet.

MOVING AIR

Warm air is lighter than cold air, so it ▶ rises. This is why hot air balloons float up into the sky. Air that has been warmed by the sun will rise up into the sky too. Sometimes you can see birds spiralling upwards on these moving air currents.

Warm air rising up in the atmosphere leaves behind an area of low pressure. Cooling as it rises, the air becomes heavy again and eventually sinks back downwards making an area of high pressure.

The sun heats the earth's surface unevenly. This creates recognizable zones of high and low pressure around the globe. ▶

Wind is simply the ▶ movement of air over the surface of the earth. Air is always being pushed out of areas of high pressure and sucked into low-pressure areas.

As a result, the world ▶ has prevailing, or regular, winds that blow between the pressure zones. Instead of blowing directly north to south between them, as you might expect, the moving air is thrown off course by the spin of the earth.

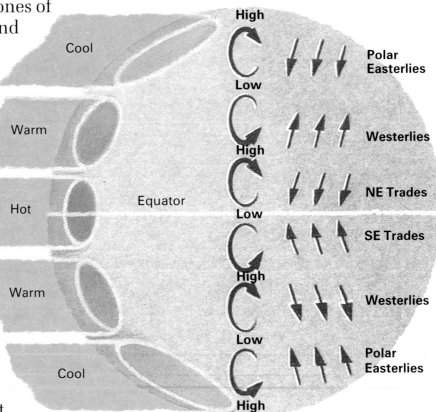

Cool — High — Polar Easterlies
Low
Warm — Westerlies
High
Hot — Equator — NE Trades
Low — SE Trades
Warm — High — Westerlies
Low
Cool — Polar Easterlies
High

1 The sun heats the earth unevenly.

2 Areas of high and low pressure are created.

3 Winds move from high to low pressure.

PRESSURE CHANGES

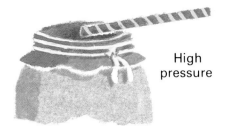

High pressure

Low pressure

There are two main types of barometer: mercury and aneroid. A mercury one measures air pressure by the height of this shiny liquid in a long thin tube. An aneroid barometer works by the movement of a flexible skin over a sealed drum. High pressure causes the skin to be pushed inwards and low pressure lets it bulge outwards.

Make a Simple Aneroid Barometer

1 Cut the neck off a balloon.
2 Stretch it tightly over a wide-necked jar and wind a rubber band or some thin string around to hold the balloon tight.
3 Use glue to stick a straw to the centre of the balloon.

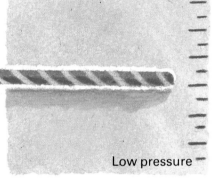

High pressure

Low pressure

4 Draw a scale on a piece of paper marked from high to low and fix this behind the end of the straw.
5 Over a number of days, watch the straw move up and down as the air pressure changes.

◀ Meteorologists can link places of the same air pressure with lines called 'isobars'. Because the isobars are drawn in at regular millibar intervals, a weather map can quickly show us the changes in air pressure. Isobars that are close together mean air pressure is changing dramatically and with this comes strong winds, whereas an area with isobars far apart will be calm.

H
1040
1032
1024
1016

1000
L

H 1008

992
984 968
L

1000
1016 1008

1016

Isobar

WINDY WEATHER

The sun's heat creates patterns of air pressure and winds in a local area as well as on a world scale.

Land always heats up and cools down more quickly than water. Because of this, hot places near the sea often have winds that vary with night and day.

▲ As the land heats air above it during the day, the warm air rises and low pressure is created. Air is sucked in from over the sea and a cool sea breeze is felt.

▲ At night, the sea is still slowly releasing its heat and warming the air above it. The situation is reversed and a cool breeze blows out to sea.

The Beaufort Scale

Force	Name of wind	Speed
0-1	Calm to light	0-5 kph
Description: Chimney smoke rises upwards or drifts slightly.		
2-3	Gentle breeze	6-20 kph
Description: Soft wind on your face. Leaves and twigs sway gently on the trees.		
4-5	Fresh breeze	21-40 kph
Description: Dust and rubbish blow along the ground. Small trees bend.		
6-7	Strong breeze	41-60 kph
Description: Big trees sway and branches toss. Washing on the line flaps.		
8-9	Gale	61-85 kph
Description: Branches snap on trees. Tiles fall from roofs. Wind is hard to walk into.		
10-11	Storm	86-120 kph
Description: People can be blown over and trees uprooted. Chimneys collapse and sheds blow over.		
12	Hurricane	Over 120 kph
Description: Houses blow down. Cars and lorries are thrown about.		

◀ At the beginning of the nineteenth century, Sir Francis Beaufort, a British admiral, worked out a scale to estimate wind speed. It is based on things that can be seen to move.

The Beaufort scale is still used today to describe wind speed. An anemometer can be used to measure the wind's speed more accurately.

Make a Weather Vane

1 Draw a large circle on to thick card. Mark on the points of the compass.

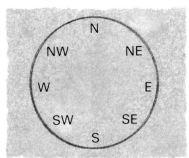

2 Use plasticine to fix a plastic pot in the middle of the circle and glue a cork to the top of the pot.

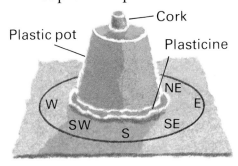

Cork
Plastic pot
Plasticine

3 Cut two triangles of card. Make one larger than the other.

4 Make slits in each end of a straw. Fit the triangles into the slits and glue them. Use the larger triangle for the tail and the smaller one for the pointer.

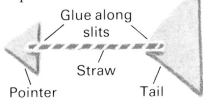

Glue along slits
Straw
Pointer
Tail

▲ A weather vane, like this one, is used to find out the direction of the wind.

5 Push a pin through the middle of the straw and then into the cork.

6 Place the wind vane outside. Use a compass or the sun to set it up in the right direction. (The sun rises in the east and sets in the west.) The wind vane will point in the direction the wind is coming from. A southerly wind will make the arrows point northwards.

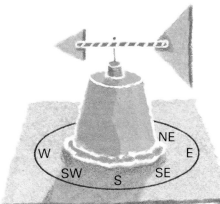

You can record your findings on a wind rose.

7 Mark the points of the compass around the edge of a piece of paper.

8 Draw a small circle in the middle.

9 Mark in rows of squares from the edge of the circle to the compass points.

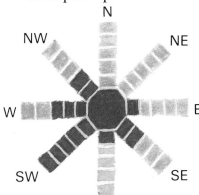

10 On different days, fill in a square on the wind rose to mark the direction of the wind.

THE WATER CYCLE

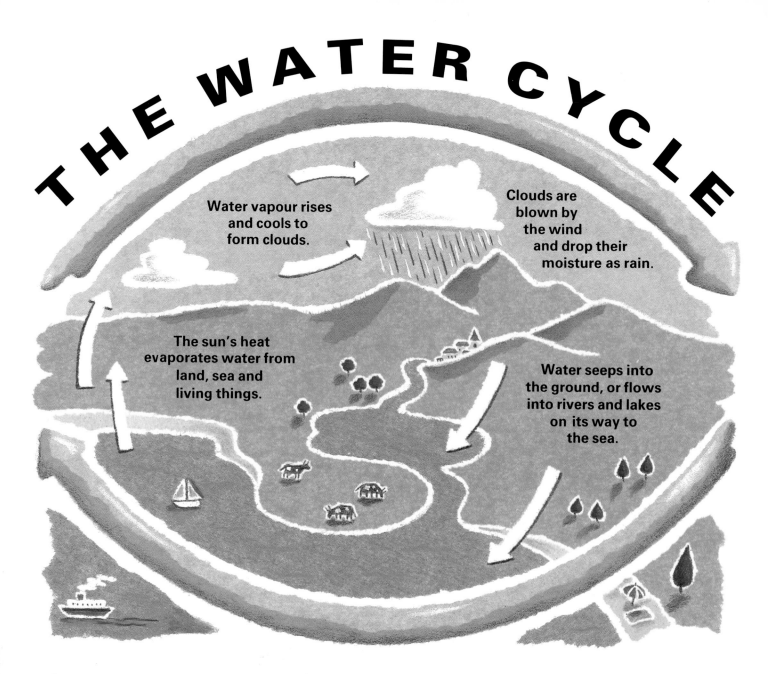

Water vapour rises and cools to form clouds.

Clouds are blown by the wind and drop their moisture as rain.

The sun's heat evaporates water from land, sea and living things.

Water seeps into the ground, or flows into rivers and lakes on its way to the sea.

There is a lot of water on earth. Most of it is salt water in the seas and oceans, and only a small amount is fresh water in lakes, rivers and underground rocks. The water cycle keeps water changing between salt and fresh water. It keeps all living things supplied with the water they need.

Heat from the sun changes water from oceans and lakes into an invisible gas called water vapour. This process is called evaporation and it takes place all the time. The water vapour rises in the atmosphere, leaving any salt in the water behind. Watch the steam from a kettle to see how water vapour rises.

As air pressure drops at high altitude, so does temperature. This makes the water vapour condense into water droplets which we see as clouds. Rain, snow or hail may fall, bringing fresh water back to earth again. Most of the water that falls over the land runs back to the seas and the water cycle starts all over again.

DEW POINT

▲ If the tiny water droplets are very fine, they may hang in the air as mist or fog. They can make it difficult to see into the distance.

If you are out on a damp, misty morning, you can often see dew drops hanging from spiders' webs. Sometimes during the night, moist air near the ground cools. The air reaches a point when it can hold no more water vapour. This is known as dew point. The water vapour turns into tiny droplets of water. These settle on grass, twigs and spiders' webs as dew.

On cold, clear nights dew point can ▶ be below freezing point which is 0° Celsius (0°C). The air cools rapidly and the water vapour forms into tiny ice crystals. Everything is covered in sparkling frost.

DAMP AIR

There is always water in the air around us, even when we can't see it as mist or fog. The exact amount depends on the temperature of the air. Warm air holds more water vapour than cold. Sometimes we can feel the moisture in warm air and we say the weather is humid.

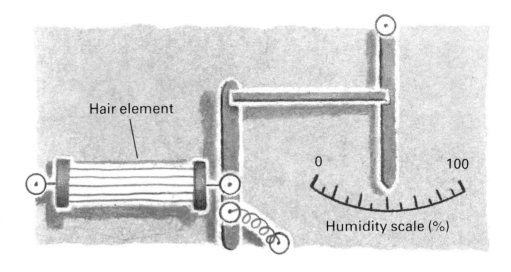

Meteorologists can actually measure the humidity, or dampness, of the air by using instruments called hygrometers.

▲ Mechanical hygrometers use hair, which stretches when wet and shrinks when dry, to move a needle on a scale.

Make a Coil Hygrometer

1 Cut a strip of card about 1 cm wide and 20 cm long, with a flap at one end.

2 Roll the card into a spiral.

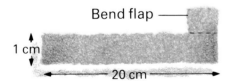

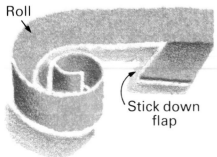

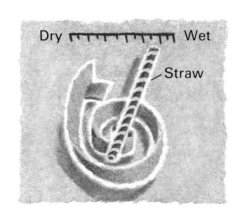

3 Bend the flap to stick the spiral on to a large piece of thick card. Don't let the spiral touch the card.

4 Fasten a straw to the end of the spiral with sticky tape.

5 Stand the hygrometer somewhere warm and dry, like over a radiator, for a few minutes. When the pointer begins to move, mark the direction with an arrow and label this 'dry'. Mark the opposite direction with an arrow and 'wet'.

6 Now leave your hygrometer in the place where you want to measure the humidity. The spiral will curl and uncurl slightly as the humidity changes.

CLOUD COVER

Clouds, like mist or fog, are made up of millions of tiny water droplets. Sometimes they may be made of tiny ice crystals too. They are formed when air full of water vapour rises into the sky and then cools. Rain may fall from the clouds as anything from a fine drizzle to a large downpour.

If you watch the clouds, you will never see two quite the same; they are always changing their shape. Even so, there are ways of describing different types of clouds. In 1803, a meteorologist called Luke Howard was the first to describe clouds by the way they look. He separated them into cirrus (meaning a tuft of hair), cumulus (meaning a heap or pile) and stratus (a flat layer). They are still described like this today, as well as by the altitude they are usually found at. ▶

Clouds at all levels usually occur at a weather front. Enormous patches of warm and cold air form over parts of the earth's surface. They are called air masses. Where warm and cold air masses meet, they don't mix but they form weather fronts instead. The warm air is pushed up into the sky and clouds appear as it rises and cools.

WOW!
The highest rainfall recorded for one day is 1870 mm on Reunion Island in the Indian Ocean on 16 March 1952.

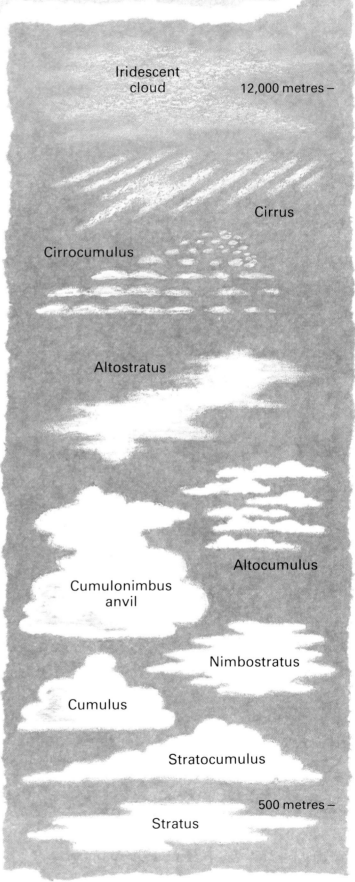

Iridescent cloud

12,000 metres –

Cirrus

Cirrocumulus

Altostratus

Altocumulus

Cumulonimbus anvil

Nimbostratus

Cumulus

Stratocumulus

500 metres –

Stratus

THUNDER AND LIGHTNING

In early times, people believed that the flash of lightning and rumble of thunder were a sign of the gods' anger. Now we know that they are simply an electrical storm.

There are about sixteen million thunderstorms a year around the world. Very often they come from dark cumulonimbus clouds that sit near to the ground and stretch right up into the sky in the shape of a blacksmith's anvil.

Water droplets and ice crystals in a thunder cloud are tossed around by movements of air. They rub together and cause the cloud to become electrically charged. When the electrical charge is great enough, it streaks between clouds or to earth as a brilliant flash of lightning.

As the electricity travels, it makes the air around it expand and then shrink very quickly. This violent movement of air creates the loud clap of thunder. When the storm is far away, the thunder rolls and rumbles as the sound is bounced between clouds. Although thunder and lightning occur at the same time, we see lightning before hearing the thunder because light travels faster than sound.

Sometimes objects on the ground may be struck by lightning and burnt, but usually thunderstorms sound more frightening than they really are.

VIOLENT STORMS

Hurricanes and tornadoes are storms that can leave behind a path of destruction and cause loss of life.

Hurricanes build up over the warm seas of the Caribbean and the south-eastern coast of North America. The sun beats down on the sea and evaporates large quantities of water. Warm, moist air rises in the atmosphere creating a large depression, or area of very low air pressure. Air is sucked in quickly to replace the rising air. A whirlpool of hot, moist air spirals around the calm centre.

▲ The hurricane grows bigger and stronger as it travels across the sea. It may measure 2000 km across and reach wind speeds of 300 kph.

◀ Tornadoes, like this one over Oklahoma in the USA, are smaller than hurricanes but their winds can reach 500 kph. They are also powered by rising humid air. The moisture condenses into water droplets so that the storm can be seen, usually as a twisting funnel shape. Tornadoes have the strength to lift heavy objects like cars and rooted trees.

WOW!
In Bedfordshire, England in May 1950 a tornado is said to have plucked the feathers off several chickens. Surprisingly, they survived their ordeal.

ICE COLD

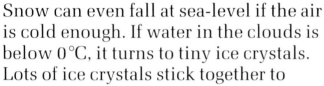

What would you pack in your case for a holiday on a mountain top? Would you take a T-shirt and shorts, expecting it to be warm up nearer the sun? In fact, being nearer the sun means the weather is colder. The thin air cannot hold as much heat as air under greater pressure nearer the earth's surface.

Snow can even fall at sea-level if the air is cold enough. If water in the clouds is below 0 °C, it turns to tiny ice crystals. Lots of ice crystals stick together to make snowflakes. When they fall through warm air, they usually turn to rain. But if they pass through cold air, fat flakes of snow will reach the ground.

▲ Some of the earth's highest mountain peaks in the Himalayas near the Equator are covered in ice and snow all year round.

Ice crystals don't always fall as snowflakes. Instead, strong winds within cumulonimbus clouds may carry ice crystals and raindrops up to the top. A layer of ice freezes around them and they fall back down. The winds can keep the crystals jogging up and down like yo-yos, building up new layers of ice each time so that small balls of ice form. When the ice balls become too heavy for the wind to lift, they fall as hailstones.

▲ Hailstones can be as small as peas but they may grow to be much larger. This photograph shows a thin section of a hailstone as big as a grapefruit. It crashed to earth in Kansas, USA, in 1970. Can you see the layers that make up the hailstone? Hailstones can damage crops and buildings. The biggest stones are big enough to kill humans and other animals.

Have you ever made an ice slide on ▶ your playground? By rubbing and polishing the ice, it can be made really smooth and slippery. Smooth surfaces create less friction, or grip, so that when you step on to the ice, the bottom of your shoe keeps sliding along. In really cold weather, ponds sometimes freeze over. Ponds don't freeze over evenly, so don't play on them in case you fall through thin ice.

CHANGING SEASONS

In parts of the world that have a temperate climate, you might expect to be able to toboggan in the cold of winter and go picnicking on warm summer days.

The seasons of the ▶ world's temperate zones are caused by the earth orbiting the sun and tilting at an angle to it. Seasons change as each half of the earth leans nearer to or away from the sun. When it is summer in the northern hemisphere it is winter in the southern hemisphere. Spring and autumn mark the changes from winter to summer and back again.

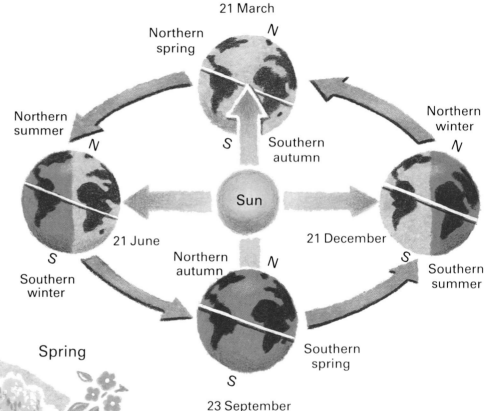

21 March
Northern spring
N
S
Southern autumn

Northern summer
N
S
Southern winter
21 June

Sun

Northern winter
N
S
Southern summer
21 December

Northern autumn
N
S
Southern spring
23 September

Winter

Spring

Autumn

Summer

◀ Trees, shrubs and small flowering plants often mark the changing seasons. New leaves and flowers appear as the air begins to warm in spring. Fruit grows, fattens and ripens during summer and contains the seeds for new plants. In autumn, many soft-leaved plants die down and deciduous trees change colour and lose their leaves before the cold of winter can harm them. The winter landscape can look bare and lifeless but the plants are ready to spring to life when the weather warms again.

MIGRATION

Some species of birds and animals migrate with the seasons. They search out rich sources of food in new parts of the world.

Some insect-eating birds follow the sunshine. Wheatears breed in Greenland in the northern summer when insects are plentiful. As autumn arrives and daylight shortens, these tiny birds fly south to find food and avoid the long cold winter in the Arctic. They fly nearly 3200 km over the sea from Greenland to the northern coast of Spain without a rest. Many continue their journey southwards to Africa. Others spend the winter in Britain or North America. ▼

▲ In the grassland area of the savannah in East Africa, seasonal changes are marked by dry and rainy periods. Vast herds of gazelle, zebra and wildebeest move 200 km between the Serengeti in the south east and the Masai Mara in the north west. They are in search of fresh green grass brought by the seasonal rains in each area.

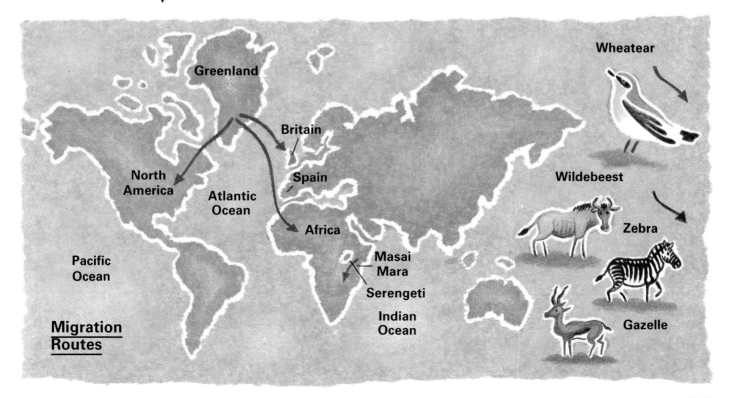

TIME AND CHANGE

Every plant and animal on earth has developed, or evolved, over millions of years to suit the climate in which they live. Their behaviour, and even the way their bodies work, will have become adapted to their surroundings.

Some animals simply hide themselves away in the cold winter months. They have eaten plenty of food during the summer and have large reserves of energy to live off. They find a snug hole or nest to fall asleep in until the weather warms up again.

◄ Sometimes the behaviour of animals has found its way into weather lore. In the USA, by tradition they mark Groundhog Day on 2 February. This is when the groundhog is supposed to come out of its long winter sleep. It seems back-to-front but if the weather is cloudy and it doesn't see its own shadow, it decides that spring is here and stays above ground. If it's sunny, it goes back into hibernation.

Mammals living in temperate and Polar areas grow thick coats to keep them warm in winter.

Stoats, like this one, ► snow-shoe hares and Arctic foxes grow white coats in winter to camouflage them against the snow. In spring they lose their thick hair and a brown coat grows to match the summer landscape. They can find just enough food to keep them going throughout the winter.

Plants have evolved to suit the climates in which they grow. In temperate regions their life cycles fit in with the seasons. They grow and reproduce during the warmer months and rest during the colder ones.

In the hot and humid climate of the Equatorial rainforests, the weather is the same all year round. Plants can be found at any stage of their life cycles at any time.

Many plants growing in hot, dry deserts have incredibly long roots that can reach down to water deep beneath the surface. Often their leaves and skins are thick and waxy to stop the precious water inside them from escaping.

▲ Some plants in deserts survive by fitting most of their life cycle into a short time after it has rained. The spring rains have brought colour to this Californian desert.

PEOPLE AND WEATHER

People have to adapt to the weather too. Take a look at the traditional clothes of people from around the world. The Innuit of the Arctic wear warm furs, while the forest dwellers of the Amazon jungle need to wear very little. How do you dress in different types of weather? ▶

◀ People living in the mountains in Morocco in northern Africa keep themselves well-wrapped up. Their long, thick clothes keep out the scorching heat of day and the bitter cold of night. Their houses have thick mud walls and tiny windows to do the same.

Houses in warm, humid lands very often don't have solid walls and roofs. Air is allowed in to cool down thè houses. In the hot, sticky climate of Pakistan, many homes are built with traps on the roof to catch wind and direct it down through the building.

Houses in cold climates need to be kept snug and warm. They are closed in with windows, doors and solid walls. Very often their roofs are insulated with fluffy material to stop heat being lost.

WOW!
In the cold Faeroes, north of Scotland, grass is grown on the roofs of the houses. This is a traditional way of insulating against heat loss.

WEATHERING

Rain, wind, frost and ice are continually changing the surface of our earth. We call these changes to the land weathering. Weathering is a very slow process. From the moment a mountain is formed by earth movements it is attacked by the weather. Over millions of years, a jagged mountain peak can be worn down.

WOW!
A mountain loses only about 8.6 cm of its height every thousand years.

▲ The Devil's Marbles in Northern Territory, Australia are a good example of 'onion skin' weathering.

Rain collects in cracks in rocks. If the weather freezes, the water expands. The ice can push the cracks in rocks apart like a wedge. Small pieces of rock, called scree, break off and often form a slope of loose material.

Wind can pick up tiny pieces of sand and throw it against rocks. It acts like a sand-blaster and the rough edges of rocks are made smooth and round.

◄ In hot deserts there is no cloud cover to protect the land from changing temperatures. Rocks bake during the day and freeze at night. This makes them expand and shrink. The outer layers of rock flake off like a peeled onion.

WOW!
Travellers in the desert say that cracking rocks make sounds like gun shots.

PREDICTING THE WEATHER

Some people look for signs around them and use old weather lore to predict the weather. Animal behaviour is said to give clues about what the weather will do. Frogs are supposed to begin to croak and sheeps' wool is said to uncurl before rain. Some plants, like sunflowers, only open in fine weather and close up before a shower. Some people keep a piece of seaweed which is hard and brittle in dry weather but becomes limp and floppy when rain is coming.

Modern weather forecasts are based on hundreds of measurements taken throughout the day. Weather stations, both on land and at sea, record temperature, rainfall, humidity, air pressure and the speed and direction of the wind.

Weather balloons carry measuring instruments into the air to gather information about the atmosphere. The readings are sent back in the form of radio waves.

WOW!
In parts of Provence in France, farmers used to keep green tree frogs under glass bells. Their croaking warned the farmers of coming rain.

In many places you will see a white box, called a Stevenson's screen, which contains weather-recording instruments. Air humidity and temperature are being recorded from this one near Mombasa in Kenya. ▼

Weather	Instruments	Units	Weather	Instruments	Units
Atmospheric pressure	Aneroid barometer	millibars	Sunshine	Campbell Stokes recorder	hours
Temperature	Thermometer	°C			
			Wind speed	Anemometer	kph
Rainfall	Rain gauge	mm	Humidity	Wet-bulb thermometer	°C

WEATHER
TECHNOLOGY

Detailed records from weather instruments have survived from as early as the seventeenth century. But it was not until 1850 that weather instruments became accurate enough to give information that could be used for forecasting. The electric telegraph, invented in the USA in 1844 by Samuel Morse, made it easy to collect readings quickly from long distances. This really helped the development of weather forecasting.

Meteorologists can now gather more information than ever by using modern technology. Satellites orbiting the earth collect weather information. They can show weather patterns that cannot be seen from earth. Satellites can even measure wind speeds at sea-level.

▲ All the information from weather stations, weather balloons, satellites and radar is fed into computers. It helps build up a picture of how the weather is changing. But there are so many different things that influence the weather, that forecasts can sometimes be inaccurate.

▲ The world's surface temperatures on a typical January day, put together from satellite data. Can you see the earth's main climatic zones (see page 7)?

CHANGING THE WEATHER

In 1946, scientists discovered that dropping tiny particles into some types of cloud could make them release rain. This became known as cloud seeding and has since been used in the USA, Russia, Australia and France. Similar methods have been used to break up fog at busy airports. In the USA, cloud seeding has also been used to try and reduce lightning in storms and in Russia it has been used to reduce the size of damaging hailstones.

Scientists would like to control the weather to help avoid natural disasters such as flooding or drought. But do they really know enough about the weather to be able to do this?

People have always wanted to be able to control the weather. Many peoples have special dances to encourage rain to fall in times of drought. Papuan mythology teaches that carrying grass during a rain dance pierces the eye of the sun, causing it to weep and be covered with clouds.

This dragon is a nineteenth-century Chinese symbol of life-bringing rain. The Dragon-Kings were called upon in times of drought or to stop flooding.

The earth's climate has changed and shifted many times during its history. As little as 10 000 years ago, a permanent layer of frozen ice was only just disappearing from northern Europe and North America as the Ice Age ended. Scientists have discovered that today's temperatures are still colder than those of millions of years ago.

People are worried that modern lifestyles are changing the world's weather. The earth is surrounded by gases in the atmosphere that act like a blanket, stopping the sun's warmth travelling back out into space (see page 6 – the greenhouse effect).

The burning of fossil fuels for energy to heat homes, run cars and keep factories working, releases the gas carbon dioxide into the atmosphere. There is now so much carbon dioxide in the atmosphere that more and more heat is being trapped.

Scientists are unsure what effects this global warming will have on the world's weather. There may be more extremes of weather like drought, flooding and hurricanes. The world's major climatic zones may even move slightly.

▲ Weather disasters, like this flooding in Mauras, India, and changes in the earth's climate are more likely to affect the poorer countries of the world. They cannot afford to take measures against the weather.

GLOSSARY

Air mass   A large body of warm or cold air.

Air pressure   The weight of atmosphere that presses down on the earth's surface.

Altitude   The height of a place above sea-level.

Anemometer   An instrument that measures wind speed.

Atmosphere   The layers of air around the earth.

Barometer   An instrument that measures air pressure.

Beaufort scale   A scale used to measure the force of the wind. It is based on observation of the effects of the wind on everyday objects.

Climate   General weather patterns experienced in a place over a long period of time.

Condense   To change from a gas into a liquid. The opposite process of evaporation.

Depression   An area of low air pressure.

Dew point   The temperature at which dew forms when water condenses out of air.

Electrical charge   A build up of positive or negative electrical particles.

Evaporate   To change from a liquid into a gas. Water changes to water vapour.

Expand   To grow bigger.

Freezing point   The temperature at which liquid water turns to solid ice. This is at 0° on the centigrade or Celsius scale.

Humidity   The amount of water vapour in the air.

Hygrometer   An instrument that measures air humidity.

Ice crystals   Tiny regular shapes of ice.

Insulation   A material that slows the passage of heat. Insulation can be used to keep things warm or cold.

Isobar   A line, drawn on a weather chart, that joins points of the same air pressure.

Life cycle   The cycle of growth, reproduction and death that all living things follow.

Meteorologist   A scientist who studies the atmosphere and weather.

Radar   A piece of equipment that uses radio waves to show on a screen how something in the atmosphere looks.

Reproduce   To produce young ones.

Water vapour   Water which is held in the air in the form of a gas.

Weather front   Where different air masses meet, usually bringing unsettled weather.

Weathering   The effect of the weather in breaking down rocks.

Weather lore   Weather sayings, myths and legends.

BOOKS TO READ

You can explore lots of topics from this book, but here is a list of other books about weather to get you started:

Autumn Weather (Seasonal Weather) by John Mason (Wayland 1990)
Be Your Own Weather Expert by Janet Kelly (Simon & Schuster 1991)
Earth in Space (Exploring Science) by Robert Stephenson and Roger Browne (Wayland 1991)
Explore the World of Weather by Robin Kerrod (Salamander 1991)
Flood (Violent Earth) by Julia Waterlow (Wayland 1992)
The Seasons by Gareth Morgan (Kingfisher 1991)
Simple Weather Experiments with Everyday Materials by Muriel Mandell (Sterling 1991)
Spring Weather (Seasonal Weather) by John Mason (Wayland 1990)
Storm (Violent Earth) by Jenny Wood (Wayland 1992)
Summer Weather (Seasonal Weather) by John Mason (Wayland 1990)
Weather (Earth Science Library) by Martyn Bramwell (Franklin Watts 1987)
Weather (Exploring Science) by Ed Catherall (Wayland 1990)
Weather and Climate (Hands on Geography) by David Flint (Franklin Watts 1991)
Weather and Climate (Science Experiments) by F Watt and F Wilson (Usborne 1991)
Weather at Work (Secrets of Science) by Robin Kerrod (Cherrytree 1992)
Weather Facts by A Ganieri (Usborne 1986)
Weather Forecaster (Be an Expert) by Barbara Taylor-Cork (Franklin Watts 1992)
The Weather Project Book by Francis Wilson (Young Headway, 1989)
Weather Projects (Science Projects) by Sharon McCormick (Cherrytree 1992)
The World's Weather (Young Geographer) by David Flint (Wayland 1992)
Wind and Weather (Science Starters) by Barbara Taylor (Franklin Watts 1991)
Winter Weather (Seasonal Weather) by John Mason (Wayland 1990)

INDEX